4/24

W9-BDN-073

Give me your tired, your poor,
your huddled masses yearning to breathe free,
the wretched refuse of your teeming shore.
Send these, the homeless, the tempest-tost...

KOREAN AMERICANS

Dale Anderson

AMERICAN IMMIGRANTS

Rourke
Publishing LLC
Vero Beach, Florida 32964

© 2008 Rourke Publishing LLC

All rights reserved. No part of this book may be reproduced or utilized in any form or by any means, electronic or mechanical including photocopying, recording, or by any information storage and retrieval system without permission in writing from the publisher.

www.rourkepublishing.com

PHOTO CREDITS: Peter Beck/Corbis: p. 30; Bettman/Corbis: pp. 14, 15; Rob Bowden/EASI-IMAGES/CFW IMAGES: p. 10; David Butow/CORBIS SABA: pp. 25, 29; County of Hawaii: p. 33; Nir Elias/Reuters/Corbis: p. 34; Emmanuel Faure/Getty Images: p. 31; Eric Foltz/Istockphoto.com: p. 8; Paul Fries/ Istockphoto.com: p. 9; Steve Geer/ Istockphoto.com: p. 17; Rob Howard/Corbis: p.43; Evan Kafka/Getty Images: p. 19; Korean Heritage Library, University of Southern California: pp. 20, 21, 35; Library of Congress: pp. 6, 13; Bernd Oberman/Corbis: p. 41; Ezio Petersen/Bettman/Corbis: p. 23; Joyce Naltchayan/AFP/Getty Images: p. 27; Paul A. Souders/Corbis: p. 40; Jim Sugar/Corbis: p. 32; Ramin Talaie/Corbis: p. 39; Chris Trotman/New Sport/Corbis: p. 36.

Cover picture shows two teenagers in a CD store [David Butow/Corbis].

Produced for Rourke Publishing by Discovery Books
Editor: Gill Humphrey
Designer: Ian Winton
Photo researcher: Rachel Tisdale

Library of Congress Cataloging-in-Publication Data

Anderson, Dale, 1953-
  Korean Americans / Dale Anderson.
      p. cm. -- (American immigrants)
  Includes bibliographical references and index.
  Audience: Grades 4-6.
  ISBN 978-1-60044-613-9
 1. Korean Americans--History--Juvenile literature. 2. Korean Americans--Social conditions--Juvenile literature. 3. Immigrants--United States--History--Juvenile literature. 4. Immigrants--United States--Social conditions--Juvenile literature. 5. United States--Emigration and immigration--Juvenile literature. 6. Korea-- Emigration and immigration--Juvenile literature. I. Title.
  E184.K6A53 2008
  973'.04957--dc22

                              2007020342

Printed in the USA

TABLE OF CONTENTS

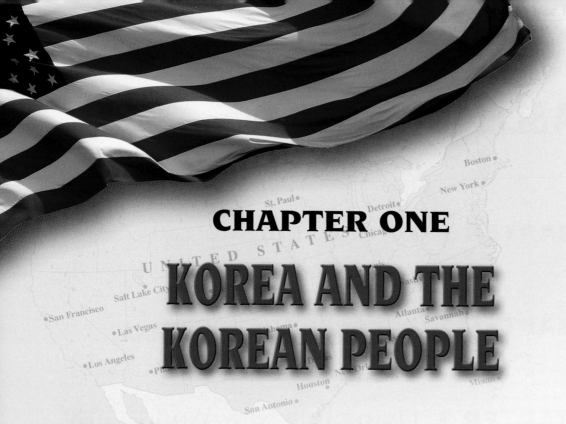

CHAPTER ONE

KOREA AND THE KOREAN PEOPLE

Korea is a **peninsula** in East Asia that sticks out from northeastern China into the sea. It is mountainous on the eastern side of the country and flatter in the west. Japan lies about 100 miles (160 km) to the east, across a narrow sea.

Foreign Influence

Throughout its history, Korea was influenced by its neighbors, China and Japan. As the first kingdoms formed in Korea, about two thousand years ago, Chinese leaders ruled a large empire known for its wealth and power. Thinkers there formed a **philosophy** called Confucianism that taught people how to live moral lives.

Koreans admired the Chinese. Korean kings and teachers wrote using Chinese **characters**. From around A.D. 400 the people began to follow Confucianism. **Buddhism**, an ancient religion that started in India, also spread to Korea from China.

(Opposite) Korea is a mountainous region, especially on the eastern side. The best soil for farming is found along the southern and western coasts.

4

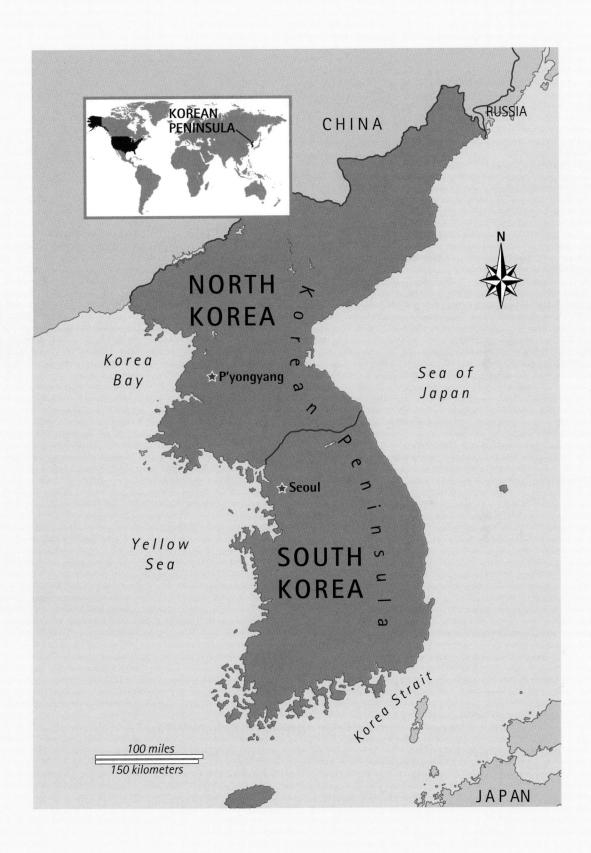

A Korean worker carries supplies under the watchful eyes of Japanese soldiers in the early 1900s.

Koreans changed some of the things they learned from China. For example, the Chinese made a beautiful green pottery called celadon. Korean potters made celadon too, but they cut designs into the pots and sometimes made them blue or tan instead of green.

Struggles with Neighbors

Korea struggled with its larger neighbors. Sometimes the Koreans fought the Chinese and Japanese to stop them taking their land. In the early 1900s, Japan gained control over Korea and ruled the land from 1910 to 1945. The Japanese ruled harshly. They took away Koreans' land, shut down Korean schools, and banned the teaching of Korean history and language.

A Divided Land

In 1945, Japan lost World War II, and its troops were forced to leave Korea. The land became divided into two countries. A **communist** leader, Kim Il Sung, led North Korea. Syngman Rhee became the ruler in South Korea. He was backed by the United States.

In 1950, North Korea's army invaded South Korea. The United States and other countries sent many soldiers to help the South Koreans. In 1953, the two sides agreed to stop fighting, but they still have not signed a peace treaty. Today, soldiers from the two Koreas patrol each side of the long fence that divides the North from the South.

Since the war, North Korea has had many problems. The government is a communist **dictatorship** that gives its people very

THE KING AND THE ALPHABET

A system of writing based on Chinese characters was used in Korea for many hundreds of years. To write, people had to learn thousands of characters. In 1440, King Sejong of Korea told teachers to develop a new way of writing. They invented an alphabet of just 24 characters that was easier to learn. This alphabet is still used in Korea today.

A South Korean soldier stands alert alongside the border between South Korea and North Korea. Thousands of soldiers patrol both sides of the border.

little freedom. The economy is poor and the country cannot produce enough food to feed everyone. At the same time large sums of money are spent on the military. Recently, the government has boasted that it has powerful **nuclear weapons**, and this has raised tension in the area.

Meanwhile, life in South Korea has improved greatly. The people there have built a strong **capitalist** economy. The government has become more **democratic**, and people enjoy more freedoms.

Korean Culture

Confucianism influenced the **culture** of Korea. Following its philosophy, fathers made all the important family decisions and wives and children did as they were told. When the oldest son in the

Seoul has been the capital of Korea since 1394. Today, more than 10 million people live there.

TANGY *KIMCHI*

The most well-known Korean dish is called *kimchi*. Koreans make *kimchi* by mixing cabbage with garlic, hot pepper, and other spices. Some kinds of *kimchi* include other vegetables, like cucumber or radishes. The mixture has to sit in a pot of baked clay for a day or two to develop the right flavor and texture! Koreans eat *kimchi* with almost every meal.

family grew up and married, he was supposed to remain in his parents' home. Today, though, young married couples are setting up their own homes, and women are demanding more freedom.

Confucianism also taught Koreans to value education. Children are expected to study hard and do well. Parents take great pride in their children's success.

(Opposite) Though Seoul is hundreds of years old, it has recently become a bustling modern city.

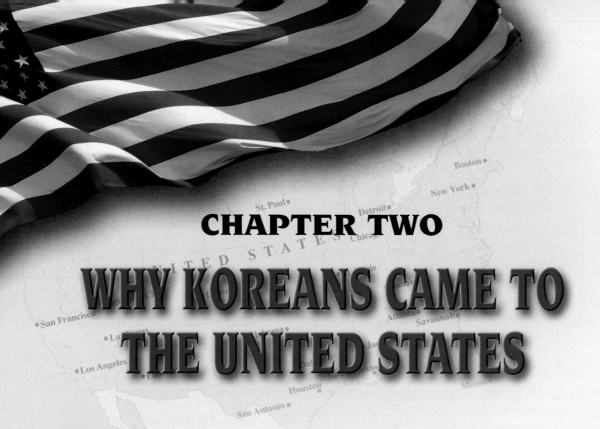

CHAPTER TWO

WHY KOREANS CAME TO THE UNITED STATES

Most Korean **immigrants** came to the United States in four different periods. About 10,000 came in the early 1900s. Around 15,000 came from about 1945 to 1960. The biggest group, more than half a million people, came from 1970 to 1990. The fourth wave, from 1991 to today, brought more than 260,000 Koreans to the United States.

The First Arrivals

The first Koreans came to the United States around 1903 to work on the sugar **plantations** in Hawaii. They came because life in Korea was difficult and they were attracted by what they heard about Hawaii. They were told the land was a paradise. The men agreed to work for three years and crossed the Pacific Ocean by ship.

A few thousand more Koreans came in the next dozen years or so. About a thousand women came to marry some of the Korean men living in Hawaii. Their families sent photos ahead so the men could identify them when their ships reached the islands. For that reason, they were called "picture brides." Nearly half of these early

An early convert to Christianity wearing traditional Korean clothes. Starting at the end of the 1700s, missionaries traveled to Korea and converted thousands of people to Christianity.

immigrants were Christians that had been converted by **missionaries** sent to Korea in the eighteenth and nineteenth centuries.

The Second Wave

The second wave of Korean immigration came from 1945 to 1960. Most were women or children. The women had married American soldiers stationed in Korea. They were called "war brides." The

SYNGMAN RHEE

At the beginning of the twentieth century, Koreans in the United States formed a group to try to gain Korea's independence from Japan. They chose Syngman Rhee as their leader. For more than twenty years, Rhee tried to convince American leaders to help Koreans gain their freedom. Later, he became the first president of South Korea.

*American General Douglas MacArthur (left) led the **United Nations (UN)** forces during part of the Korean War. Here he talks with Syngman Rhee, the president of South Korea.*

children were often orphans who were adopted by American families.

Some of these immigrants continued to come by ship. Others crossed the Pacific Ocean by plane. They typically traveled alone or in small groups, wondering what new life they would find in the United States.

According to news reports of the 1950s, Yoong Soon (left) was the first Korean woman to marry an American soldier. Later, she and her husband, Sergeant John Morgan of the U.S. Army, had the first Korean-American child coming from a war-bride marriage.

A PLANE JOURNEY TO THE UNITED STATES

Imjung Kwuon came to the United States on a plane in 1962: "I remember that I didn't know what was happening. I just remember me and my younger sister causing a lot of trouble on the plane, making noise, crying—I was so unhappy, and the food tasted awful."

From 1945 onward, nearly all immigrants came from South Korea. Even today, it is almost impossible for North Koreans to escape their country. Those that do, live as **refugees** in China.

Surge in Immigration

The biggest surge in immigration from South Korea took place in the 1970s and 1980s. During these twenty years, around 30,000 people came to the United States each year. This was because in 1965,

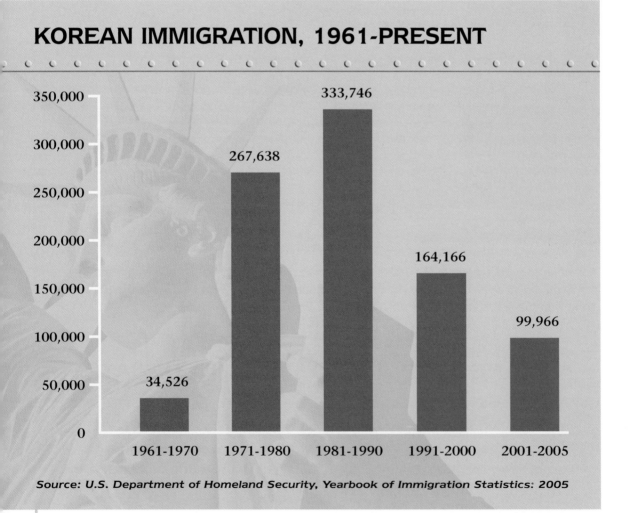

KOREAN IMMIGRATION, 1961-PRESENT

Source: U.S. Department of Homeland Security, Yearbook of Immigration Statistics: 2005

This graph shows the number of Korean immigrants arriving in the U.S. after 1961. Before 1961, just over 20,000 Koreans came to the United States.

Most South Koreans live in cities, but some still live in rural areas and make a difficult living by farming the land.

Congress passed a new law about immigration. It allowed many thousands more people to come to the United States each year. It also made it easier for people to come to the U.S. to join family members already there. Because of this, the "war brides" could bring their parents, brothers, and sisters.

Tens of thousands of Koreans came to the United States in search of better lives and good jobs. Others, especially women, came because they wanted more freedom and greater opportunities. About 13,000 Korean doctors and nurses came to the U.S. between 1965 and 1979.

Immigration Since 1990

Since 1990, immigration from Korea has slowed. Only about 16,000 people come each year. One reason is that life in South Korea has improved greatly. The economy has grown much stronger, and people have more freedoms than in the past.

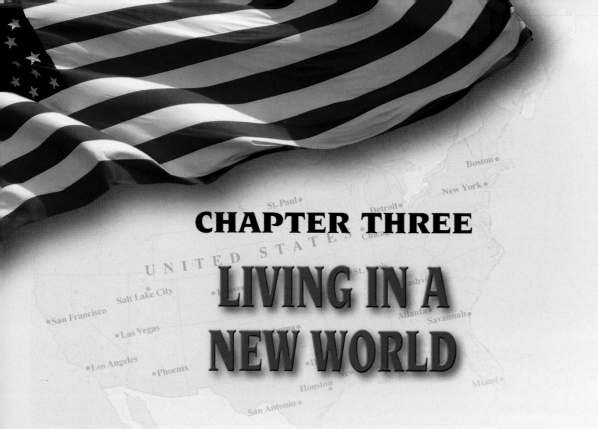

CHAPTER THREE
LIVING IN A NEW WORLD

The United States is very different from Korea. The language, **customs**, and beliefs of the American people often seem strange to Korean immigrants, and they have sometimes struggled to adapt. Americans themselves have not always accepted Koreans or other Asian immigrants.

Life in the Early 1900s

Korean immigrants working on the Hawaiian sugar plantations had to labor in the sugarcane fields ten hours every day, six days a week. They got only a ten-minute lunch break. The Korean workers had agreed to work for three years, and when they finished some left Hawaii for California.

There, some settled in cities like Los Angeles and San Francisco. They often worked in restaurants, or as gardeners or servants. Some saved or borrowed money to open shops. However, most Korean Americans worked as farm laborers. They formed groups of ten workers who went from farm to farm picking fruits and vegetables. Often they pooled their earnings so they could help each other buy land.

Koreans joined workers from China, Japan, the Philippines, and other countries to work in the vast sugarcane fields of Hawaii in the late 1800s and early 1900s.

Life in the Middle 1900s

The Korean-American community remained small throughout the 1960s. In 1940, only about 2,000 Korean Americans lived in mainland United States. They formed churches, which became

*Most Korean Americans who were Christians belonged to **Protestant** churches, like these **Methodists** pictured here outside their church in 1950. It was Protestants who had sent missionaries to Korea.*

important centers of social life as well as religious worship. The churches set up social groups for young people. Members who knew how to read and write in English taught those skills to those who did not. Members of the same church helped each other face the difficulties of life in the United States.

KOREAN AMERICANS DURING WORLD WAR II

During World War II, Korean Americans threw themselves into the war effort. They hoped that an American victory would lead to independence for their **homeland**. Many Korean Americans knew the Japanese language. They translated captured documents and taught the language to other soldiers. Many young Korean-American men served in the army.

In 1944, Young Oak Kim is awarded the Silver Star medal for his heroic actions during World War II.

Yanny Rhee came to the United States in 1963 to join an older brother:

"My first year in the U.S. was very hard. I could read and write some English, but I couldn't understand what people were saying, and I could not speak. So I just smiled at people all the time.... What could I do? I didn't know what they were asking me, and I couldn't say anything."

Life in the 1970s and 1980s

Starting around 1970, Koreans began coming to the United States in larger numbers. Most settled along the west coast, especially in California. Koreatown in Los Angeles became very large, as more and more Korean immigrants settled there. Tens of thousands of Korean Americans went to live in New York City and New Jersey.

Korean Americans opened grocery stores and nail salons. They started dry cleaning businesses and clothing stores. Some were located in areas like Koreatown and mainly served Korean Americans. Others were found in different neighborhoods. These businesses did not only help the owner. They also gave jobs to other members of the family or to recent arrivals from Korea.

(Opposite) A Korean American setting up a display in front of his store in 1985. Korean Americans formed lending groups called kyes. *Members pooled their money, and then some borrowed it to start their own businesses. When they paid the money back, it was available for other members of the kye to borrow.*

RACE DISCRIMINATION

Dong Hwan Ku came to the United States from Korea in 1984. He spoke of his frustration with life in the United States:
"When I compare the dream I had of America with the reality, I know this is not an easy country to live in. When I finish paying off my debts, I hope I can go back to Korea....It is very hard to live as an immigrant here....Race discrimination is far too strong....I am sick and tired. I feel defeated."

Outbreak of Violence

Korean Americans suffered a shock in the early 1990s. Many of those who lived in Los Angeles had businesses in areas where African Americans lived. People from the two groups did not always get along well.

African Americans in Los Angeles were at the city's police department. They were angry because the city police officers had beaten a black man. The anger boiled over on April 29, 1992, when a riot broke out. Some African Americans took goods from Korean-

WORKING WITH THE BLACK COMMUNITY

Tong Sun Lim is a church minister who lives in Los Angeles:
"I am optimistic about the future of race relations....One of our deacons has a grocery store in a black community. He employs many black people, who take charge of the store when he goes out. He attends the black church and sometimes teaches Sunday school....When the riots occurred, his neighbors guarded the store."

After the Los Angeles riots in 1992 thousands of Asian Americans, including many Korean Americans, marched in favor of building better relations between the races.

American stores and attacked the owners. The riot left more than 2,300 Korean-American businesses destroyed. As a result Korean Americans began trying to build bridges to people in other groups.

CHAPTER FOUR
KOREAN AMERICANS TODAY

About 1.1 million Korean Americans live in the United States. They are found in every state, though about half live in the west. More than four out of five were born in Korea and many speak Korean as well as English. The great majority of Korean Americans are Christians.

KOREAN NAMES

There are around 250 family names in use in Korea, but a few very common names are shared by more than half of all Koreans. The three most popular are Kim, Lee, and Park. In Korea, family names are listed first, followed by a two-syllable personal name. Many Korean Americans adopt the western style and put the family name last. In Korea, women do not change their family name when they marry. However, many Korean-American women do take their husband's name.

Korean-American students study hair styling in the hopes of opening their own beauty salons one day. The desire to own one's own business is still strong in the Korean-American community.

The impact of Koreans' emphasis on education is clear. More than one out of four Korean Americans has a college degree or higher. For Americans in general, the number is fewer than one in six. Still, a large number of Korean Americans are struggling. Nearly one in six lives in poverty.

In and Out of Koreatown

Many poorer Korean Americans live in Koreatowns like the one in Los Angeles. Stores, shops, and restaurants advertise with signs in Korean. The tempting smell of Korean barbecue and other tasty foods fills the air. So does Korean music. Clubs often have **karaoke**, which Korean Americans really enjoy. Koreatowns attract visitors from outside the area.

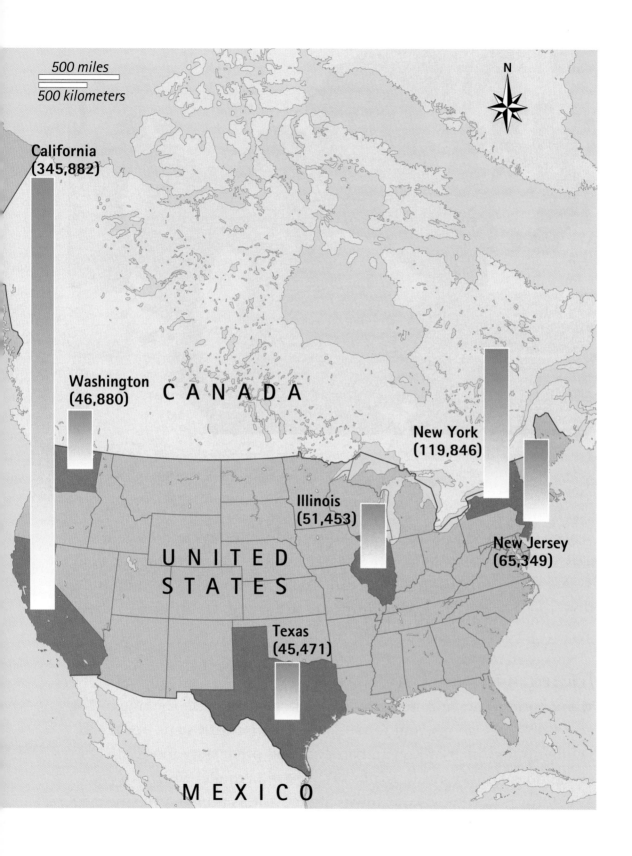

500 miles
500 kilometers

N

California
(345,882)

Washington
(46,880)

C A N A D A

New York
(119,846)

Illinois
(51,453)

U N I T E D
S T A T E S

New Jersey
(65,349)

Texas
(45,471)

M E X I C O

28

Shops and a food court bring business to a modern shopping mall in the Koreatown of Los Angeles. Other businesses are found along the streets of the district.

Many Korean Americans with more education work as doctors, lawyers, or engineers. They have higher incomes and live in larger homes in the suburbs.

Different Generations

Korean Americans call people who came to the United States as adults the "first generation." Those who came as children, they call the "1.5 generation." The children of immigrants are called the "second generation." Many in the first generation found it harder to adapt to American life. They had more difficulty learning English and adjusting to American ways. Their children have fewer memories of life in Korea and have adopted American culture more easily. Sometimes parents and children clash over matters like dating. Some parents insist that their children learn the Korean language.

(Opposite) This map shows the states with the most Korean Americans. About one in three of all Korean Americans lives in California. Another one in ten lives in New York.

Some Korean Americans use their knowledge of the Korean language to conduct business in South Korea, although many businesspeople in South Korea speak English also.

Keeping Traditions

Korean Americans have kept many traditions alive. Many Korean-American families celebrate each child's first birthday, a special occasion in Korea. Children are dressed in traditional Korean clothes and given specially-made rice cakes to eat. Parents put objects like rice, a book, a bow and arrow, and a ruler in front of the child. The one he or she touches first is thought to predict the child's future.

Children honor their parents, too. They stage a special feast when parents reach their sixtieth birthday. Dozens of guests are invited and when the party begins, each guest takes a turn bowing to the person being honored. Another highlight is when the oldest son puts the birthday parent on his back and dances. The dance shows respect for his parent on reaching a milestone in life.

THE KOREAN FAMILY

Journalist K.W. Lee talked, in the early 1990s, about the importance of the family to Korean Americans:
"The Korean family...is the main source of energy and passion, of energy and discipline, for Koreans in America....I call it the 'piggy-back syndrome': the children on the parents' backs are continually aware that they must lighten their parents' burden by succeeding in school."

A Korean-American couple poses with their young baby. Korean Americans tend to have smaller families than was traditionally the case in Korea.

CHAPTER FIVE

CONTRIBUTING TO AMERICAN CULTURE

Do you enjoy biting into a juicy nectarine? If so, thank Kim Chong-nim, who had a large farm in California in the early 1900s. Workers for his company developed the first nectarine or perhaps you can learn tae kwon do. That martial art was developed in Korea.

Politicians and Scientists

In recent years, Korean Americans have become more involved in politics. In 2000, Harry Kim was elected the mayor of the largest island in the state of Hawaii. Herbert Choy (1916-2004) was the son of Korean immigrants. In 1971, he became the first Asian American to be named a federal judge.

Many Korean Americans have done important work in science and medicine. Suk Ju Hong did work that helped lead to laser printing. Jim Yong Kim, a doctor, helped start a group called Partners in Health. It works to improve the health of poor people around the world.

HARRY KIM

In 2005, Mayor Harry Kim talked about what he learned from his parents:
"Immigrants are willing to sacrifice anything just for a shot at the kind of lifestyle we have....And hardships of any kind were merely bumps in the road in reaching their goals of a life for their families."

(Right) Harry Kim is mayor of the County of Hawaii, the largest island in Hawaii. Fewer than 25,000 Korean Americans live in the County of Hawaii today.

(Opposite) The Korean martial art of tae kwon do trains students to defend themselves using both legs and arms. It has become very popular in the United States.

Sarah Chang rehearses here as she prepares for a concert with a symphony orchestra. A leading violinist once called her "the most wonderful, the most perfect, the most ideal violinist I have ever heard."

Entertainers

Four young Korean women have gained great success playing classical music. Sarah Chang (1980-) began playing the violin when she was only three. By age eight, she was invited to play with leading orchestras. Now in her twenties, she has played with orchestras around the world. The Ahn Trio are three Korean-American sisters. Critics rave about their playing.

Three Korean Americans have found success on television. Sandra Oh (1971-) stars in the medical drama *Gray's Anatomy*. Daniel Dae Kim (1968-) and Yunjin Kim (1973-) star in the thriller *Lost*. In 2006, all three won Screen Actors Guild awards for their work.

Athletes

Several Korean-American athletes have become famous. The first was Sammy Lee (1920-), a diver who won gold medals in diving at the 1948 and 1952 Olympic Games. This made him the first Asian American to win a gold medal.

Sammy Lee was a doctor in the U.S. Army when he won his first gold medal for diving in 1948. After winning his second gold medal in 1952, he won the Sullivan Award, given to the country's best amateur athlete.

HINES WARD'S JOURNEY

In 2006, Hines Ward returned to South Korea on a mission. Tens of thousands of people there, like him, had one Korean parent and one parent from another race. These people suffer from unfair treatment in South Korea. Ward wanted to convince South Koreans to change their attitudes. His mission won praise from newspapers and attention from government leaders.

Michelle Wie (1989-) started playing golf when she was only 4 years old. In her teens, she became a professional golfer. She mostly competed against women, but in 2004 she reached the finals in a men's tournament.

Hines Ward (1976-) has a Korean mother and an African-American father. He began playing for the Pittsburgh Steelers in the National Football League in 1998. Ward set many team records as a receiver. In 2006, he helped the Steelers win Super Bowl XL and won the game's Most Valuable Player award.

(Opposite) Michelle Wie has impressed golf experts with her long, powerful drives.

CHAPTER SIX

THE FUTURE FOR KOREAN AMERICANS

In 2003, Korean Americans celebrated one hundred years of life in the United States. Much had changed since the first few thousand Koreans arrived in Hawaii. Now they live in every state and work in many different jobs.

A TRADITIONAL RECIPE

Andrea Kim, like many Korean Americans, sees traditional food as a way of celebrating her **heritage**:

"Whenever we had a family get together, we would have Korean food. My mother would make Korean marinated beef....I learned how to make that by going to the family gatherings....So now when I entertain, the greatest compliment I can show my guests is to serve Korean food....I was very close to my grandmother, and she taught me how to make it."

Young dancers perform on the streets of New York City during a Korean Day parade.

Immigration in the Future

It is hard to say how many Koreans will come to the United States in the future. If the economy of South Korea remains strong, and people have enough freedom, they are less likely to leave their homeland. However, the situation with North Korea might change. North and South Korea may start fighting again or the communist government in the north may collapse. This would lead to uncertainty and change that could have an impact on Korean immigration.

Korean-language signs can still be found in many shops and stores owned by Korean Americans.

Changing Patterns

The lives of Korean Americans will probably change. This is especially true for Korean Americans born in the U.S. who marry non-Koreans. They will have families where only one parent is of Korean descent and so the influence of Korean culture will be weaker.

Work life could change in the future also. Both the 1.5 generation and the second generation are less likely than the first generation to own their own small businesses. This is partly because many Korean Americans have a better education than their parents. They remember the hardship and long working hours that their parents endured, and want a different life for themselves.

On an outdoor screen, Korean Americans watch South Korea compete against France during the 2006 soccer World Cup. Rooting for the national team during international sporting events is one way Korean Americans keep in touch with their homeland.

ONE HUNDRED PERCENT KOREAN AMERICAN

Youn Jae Kim came to the United States in 1988:
"Many people ask me whether I want to go back to Korea or stay here. I think this is not the issue anymore....I can't be 100 percent Korean or 100 percent American. But at the same time, I can be *both* 100 percent Korean *and* 100 percent American."

Challenges and Hopes

Korean Americans have had to face many challenges. People from other racial groups have not always accepted them. They have been blocked at schools and jobs by unfair treatment. Today, even well-educated Korean immigrants sometimes have to take poorer jobs because employers ignore the education they received in Korea.

The Los Angeles riots of 1992 scarred the Korean-American community. Many Korean Americans worked to turn that tragic event into something good. They became more politically active so they could have a stronger voice in their communities. They have done more to connect with people in other groups.

At the same time, Korean Americans feel strong ties to each other. They treasure their common heritage and feel proud of their own culture and all it has produced. They will want to carry that pride into the future.

(Opposite) Korean Americans maintain many traditions, but many also enjoy American culture, like these newlyweds who are munching on hot dogs in New York's Central Park.

GLOSSARY

Buddhism (BOO diz uhm) — religion and philosophy that was founded in India in the sixth century. It spread to Central Asia, China, Korea, and Japan

capitalist (KAP uh tuh list) — economic system in which people can start their own businesses and keep the profits they earn

characters (KA rik turs) — letters, marks, or symbols, used in writing

communist (KOM yuh nist) — economic system in which the government owns all businesses and decides all wages and prices

culture (KUHL chur) — way of life of a group of people, including their language, beliefs, and arts, their styles of housing, dressing, and cooking

customs (KUHSS tuhms) — a traditional way of behaving

democratic (dem uh KRAT ik) — a form of government where the people vote for their own leaders

dictatorship (DIK tay tur ship) — country or government ruled by a dictator. The dictator has complete power over his or her people

discrimination (diss krim i NAY shuhn) — unfair treatment

heritage (HER uh tij) — the customs and traditions handed down from generation to generation

homeland (home land) — the country where a person is born, or where their family, or ancestors lived

immigrant (IM uh gruhnt) — person who has moved from another country to start a new life

karaoke (kah ree OH kee) — a form of entertainment in which people sing the words to popular songs while a machine plays the background music

Methodist (METH uhd ist) — a Protestant-Christian group based on the teachings and work of John and Charles Wesley and others in the eighteenth century

missionaries (MISH uh ner ees) — religious people who travel abroad to try to convince others to join their religion

nuclear weapon (NOO klee ur WEP uhn) — a bomb that can kill a huge number of people very quickly

peninsula (puh NIN suh luh) — land that is largely surrounded by sea

philosophy (fuh LOSS uh fee) — system of thinking that tries to explain how people should behave

plantation (plan TAY shuhn) — large farms where large numbers of workers grow crops like sugar, cotton, or tobacco. These crops are then sold for profit

Protestants (PROT uh stuhnts) — Christians that belong to churches that are not Roman Catholic or Orthodox

refugees (ref yuh JEES) — people that are forced to leave their homes or countries because of war or persecution

United Nations (UN) (yoo NI tid NAY shuhns) — an international organization set up to promote world peace

FURTHER INFORMATION

Places to Visit or Write

Korean American Museum
3727 West 6th Street, Suite 400
Los Angeles, CA 90020
213-388-4229

Korean Cultural Center
5505 Wilshire Blvd.
Los Angeles, CA 90036
323-936-7141

Korean Cultural Service
460 Park Ave.
New York, NY 10022
212-759-9550

Books

Korean Americans. Scott Ingram. World Almanac Library, 2007.

Korean Americans: The New Immigrants. Anne Soon Choi. Chelsea
House Publications, 2007.

South Korea (Countries of the World series). Lucile Davis. Capstone
Press, 2006.

Websites to Visit

www.koreak12.org//index.php?option=com_docman&Itemid=26
Material on the history and culture of Korea.

www.lifeinkorea.com
Has information on Korean history and culture in the "Culture & Language" section.

Video

Korean-American Heritage. Schlessinger Media, 2006.

CD-ROMS

Korea: A Cultural Bouquet. Samsung Cultural Foundation.

INDEX